Date:

To:

As you use this book to study the Word, confess and pray this year, may you become a thousand times more than your fathers."

From:

I BELIEVE and CONFESS...

KNOWING AND CONFESSING HIS WORD

Volume 2

ANDY YAWSON

Published by :

Illumination House

P.O. Box DS1277 - Dansoman - Accra - Ghana

Email: illumination_house@yahoo.com

Printed in Ghana

ISBN 978-9988-2-0791-5

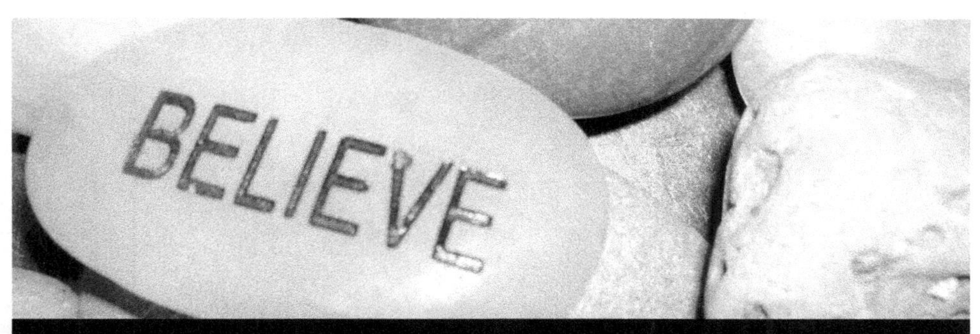

TABLE OF CONTENTS

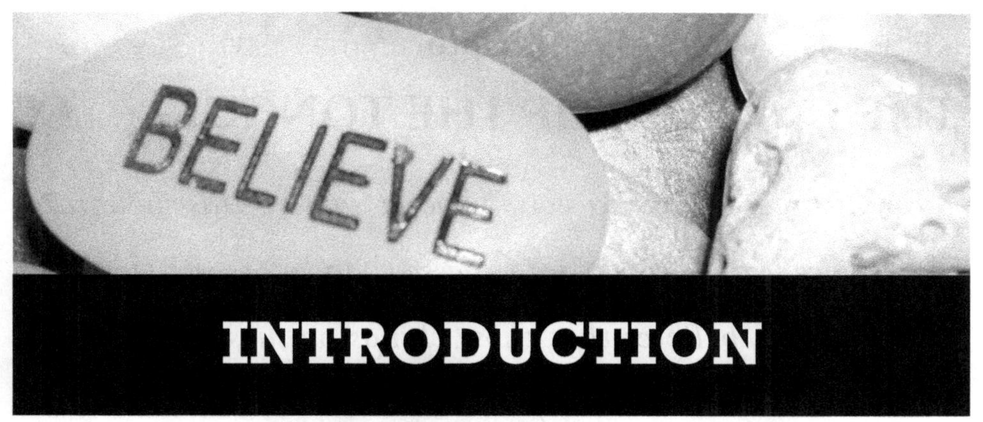

INTRODUCTION

Do you sometimes wonder how some people achieve great things in adverse conditions? Have you come across some who appear to thrive in spite of great opposition?

One thing that seems to be consistent in the lives of such overcomers is what they say to themselves, even when everyone else may be criticising or walking away.

The Bible places much value on the role of the tongue in our lives.

It shows us that as much as it is important for us to believe the word of God, the faith that is generated by knowing and believing the word of God cannot remain silent. It ought to speak because the words will put the faith to action.

This is what the scripture has to say on:-

THE PURPOSE OF THE TONGUE

"For assuredly, I say to you, whoever says to this mountain, 'Be removed and be cast into the sea,' and does not doubt in his heart, but believes that those things he says will be done, he will have whatever he says." **Mark 11:23**

After one has believed, it is the words that puts the faith to action - 'whatever he says'

THE POWER OF THE TONGUE

"Death and life are in the power of the tongue, And those who love it will eat its fruit." **Proverbs 18:21**

The tongue is so powerful that it can cut both ways and you and I are to choose what we want to use our word for - death or life.

THE PRODUCT OF THE TONGUE

"A man's stomach shall be satisfied from the fruit of his mouth; From the produce of his lips he shall be filled." **Proverbs 18:20**

Your word can actually determine what eventually comes to you - you shall be filled with the produce of your lips.

Having established all these, you will agree with me that it is time we started actively finding out what God's word says about us and confessing it in order to reap the fruit of those words.

This book is intended to assist you in achieving exactly that. Learn at least a scripture a week, make Bible-based confessions and back them up with prayer.

God bless you as you make this your weekly routine!

1st to 7th January

THE FUTURE

SCRIPTURE FOR THE WEEK

"A man's stomach shall be satisfied from the fruit of his mouth, From the produce of his lips he shall be filled." **Proverbs 18:20**

CONFESSION

- I believe and confess that I serve a living God and as I declare my future by faith, I will experience it as declared in Jesus name.
- I declare and decree that in January, the Lord will show Himself strong on my behalf. In February, the peace of God and abundant joy will rest in my home in the name of Jesus.
- Divine encounters will be my portion in March and major doors will open for me in the month of April.

- I declare today that unusual testimonies will meet me in May and in June I shall experience the manifestation of His power in my personal life.
- The Lord will cause me to reap a great harvest in July and there shall be all-round progress in every area of my life in August.
- Supernatural breakthroughs will be my experience in September and I will operate under open heavens throughout October.
- November will be a season of God's favour in my life and the month of December shall be full of thanksgiving.
- I declare today that I am blessed and highly favoured.

PRAYER POINTS FOR THE WEEK

- Pray in the name of Jesus that the Lord will continually show Himself strong on your behalf.
- Pray that the peace of God and abundant joy will rest in your home in the name of Jesus.

- Pray that you shall experience the manifestation of His power in your personal life.
- Thank God that your future will be an experience of Supernatural breakthroughs in the name of Jesus.

SCRIPTURE FOR THE WEEK

"My covenant I will not break, nor alter the word that has gone out of My lips. Once I have sworn by My holiness; I will not lie to David." **Psalms 89:34-35**

CONFESSION

- I believe and confess that I serve a covenant-keeping God. No word that He has spoken over my life will fall unfulfilled.
- I declare today that the promises of God will not fail in any area of my life.
- All the days of my life, I will be a living testimony of the faithfulness of God. His glory will manifest more and more in my life in the name of Jesus.

- I confess that I receive grace to be a covenant-keeper. I receive grace to be a person of integrity.
- I declare and decree that no storm or negative circumstance will hinder me from walking into the manifestation of what God has promised me.
- As I step into this week, I declare that nothing will cause me to take my eyes off God's word. I receive testimonies from every side, in the name of Jesus.
- I declare today that I am blessed and highly favoured.

PRAYER POINTS FOR THE WEEK

- Pray in the name of Jesus that the promises of God concerning every area of your life will be fulfilled.
- Pray in the name of Jesus that all the days of your life, the Lord will cause His glory to manifest more and more in your life.
- Ask the Lord to give you grace to be a covenant keeper just as He is in Jesus name.

- Thank God that every word that He has spoken over your life will be fulfilled in the name of Jesus.

SCRIPTURE FOR THE WEEK

"Live such good lives among the pagans that, though they accuse you of doing wrong, they may see your good deeds and glorify God on the day he visits us."
1 Peter 2:12

CONFESSION

- I believe and confess that the Lord is my Maker and He has made me in His own image.
- I confess that all the days of my life, I will reflect His glory. I declare that the Lord's will, will be done in all my dealings.
- I decree that from this day, the Lord reigns in every area of my life.
- I confess that from today men will see what God

is doing through me and glorify God. I am a living testimony of the grace of God.

- Men and women will turn to God when they see the transformation that God is bringing into my life.
- I declare today that I am blessed and highly favoured.

PRAYER POINTS FOR THE WEEK

- Thank the Lord for making you in His own image.
- Pray in the name of Jesus for the grace to reflect God's glory all the days of your life.
- Ask the Lord to continually reign in every area of your life as you surrender all to Him.
- Pray that through the transformation that God is bringing into your life, many will turn to God.

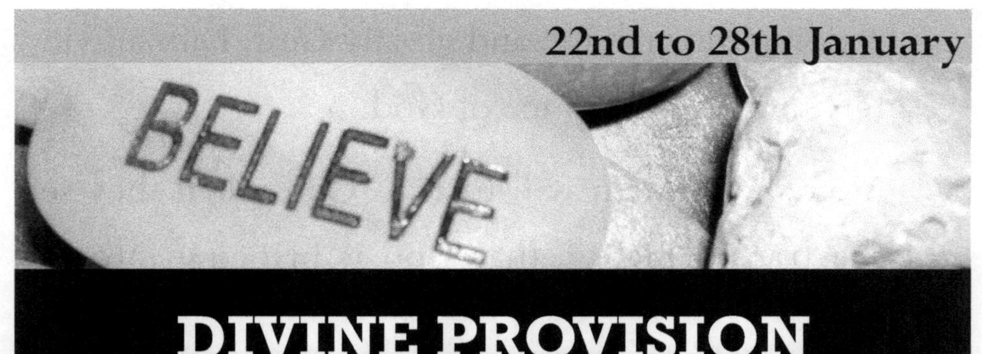

SCRIPTURE FOR THE WEEK

"The Lord will guide you continually, And satisfy your soul in drought, And strengthen your bones; You shall be like a watered garden, And like a spring of water, whose waters do not fail." **Isaiah 58:11**

CONFESSION

- I believe and confess that the heavens over my life is opened in Jesus name.
- As I step into this month, I declare that I will experience all round release in my life in the name of Jesus.
- Anything that is blocking or delaying my blessing is removed in the name of Jesus.

- I receive uncommon favour in every area of my life.
- I declare and decree that I have stepped into a new season in my life now. From today, I will experience divine supply even in the midst of drought.
- My experience here on earth will be directly influenced by heaven in the name of Jesus.
- I confess today that I am walking into abundance of wealth, abundance of peace, abundance of joy and an abundance of God's protection and His presence over my life.
- I am a walking testimony from this day onwards.
- I declare today that I am blessed and highly favoured.

PRAYER POINTS FOR THE WEEK

- Pray in the name of Jesus that this week you will experience all round release in your life.
- In the name of Jesus, command anything that is blocking or delaying your blessing to be removed.

- Pray in the name of Jesus that together with your household, you will experience divine supply even in the midst of drought.
- Thank God that you are walking into abundance of wealth, abundance of peace, abundance of joy and an abundance of His protection.

VICTORIOUS LIVING

SCRIPTURE FOR THE WEEK

" For the weapons of our warfare are not carnal but mighty in God for pulling down strongholds, casting down arguments and every high thing that exalts itself against the knowledge of God, bringing every thought into captivity to the obedience of Christ." **2 Corinthians 10:4-5**

CONFESSION

- I believe and confess that the Lord is my strength and He has become my salvation.
- I declare today that I walk under the grace and protection of God. No weapon formed against me will prosper.
- I declare and decree that no storm or challenge will stop me from rising to the top. No attack of

the enemy or delays in my expectation will hinder my growth in God. I confess today that my expectation will not be cut off in the name of Jesus.

- I believe and confess that I continually walk in the authority that God the Father has given me. In the name of Jesus, the name that is above every name, I establish victory in every area of my life.
- I declare that by the blood of Jesus, I rise above any negative covenants that will attempt to attack any area of my life. As I walk by faith, in the word of God and prayer, I declare that every chain of bondage in my life is broken. I am free in the name of Jesus.
- I declare today that I am blessed and highly favoured.

PRAYER POINTS FOR THE WEEK

- Pray in the name of Jesus that you will continually walk in the authority that God the Father has given you.

- Pray in the name of Jesus that no storm or challenge will stop you from rising to the top.
- Pray in the name of Jesus, and establish victory in every area of your life.
- Thank God, that by the name that is above every name you are rising above any negative covenants that will attempt to attack any area of your life.

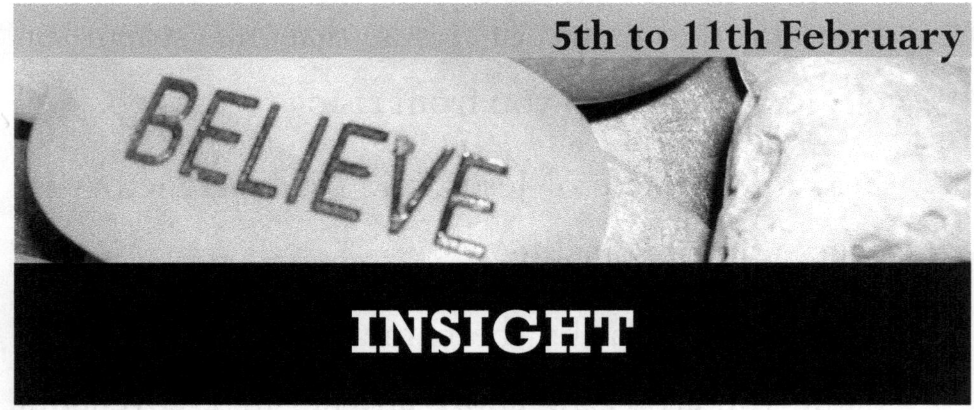

SCRIPTURE FOR THE WEEK

"Through wisdom a house is built, and by understanding it is established; by knowledge the rooms are filled with all precious and pleasant riches." **Proverbs 24:3-4**

CONFESSION

- I believe and confess that the Lord is good and merciful unto me.
- I declare based on His word that He has given me all that pertains to life and godliness. I confess today that I will not live in ignorance concerning the power, the authority and the blessing that God has given me through Christ Jesus.
- I declare that from today, I will seek to know what the word of God says concerning every area of my

life. I refuse to yield any territory of my life to the devil through ignorance, in the name of Jesus.

- I confess that my eyes are opened to know what the hope of His calling is concerning my life. I possess every territory that God has marked for me in the name of Jesus.
- I declare that the walls of ignorance are coming down in every area of my life in the name of Jesus.
- I declare today that I am blessed and highly favoured.

PRAYER POINTS FOR THE WEEK

- Pray in the name of Jesus, that the Lord will give you insight as you seek to know what the word of God says concerning every area of your life.
- Pray in the name of Jesus for the grace to never yield any territory of your life to the devil through ignorance or any act of deception.
- In the name of Jesus, secure by the shed blood of the Lamb every territory that God has marked for

you and your household.

- Thank God that your eyes are opened to know what the hope of His calling is concerning your life.

LIVING OUT YOUR ORIGINAL PURPOSE

SCRIPTURE OF THE WEEK

"Let us hear the conclusion of the whole matter: Fear God, and keep his commandments: for this is the whole duty of man. For God shall bring every work into judgment, with every secret thing, whether it be good, or whether it be evil."

Ecclesiastes 12:13-14

CONFESSION

- I believe and confess that I am created to show the praises of my God. I declare that every area of my life will reflect the glory of God.
- From this day onwards, I confess that I will be the evidence of the goodness and glory of God.
- My spiritual life, my business life, my career and my family life will reflect the glory of God. My

thoughts, my speech and my actions will all declare the glory of God.

- I believe and confess that major testimonies are breaking out in my life. Great and unusual testimonies are my portion in Jesus name.
- Every area of battle in my life will become a reason for celebration. I declare and decree that in all things I am more than a conqueror.
- I declare today that I am blessed and highly favoured.

PRAYER POINTS FOR THE WEEK

- Pray in the name of Jesus for the grace to always show the praises of God in all you do.
- Pray in the name of Jesus that every area of your life will reflect the glory of God.
- Pray in the name of Jesus that every area of battle in your life will become a reason for celebration.
- Thank the Lord that great and unusual testimonies are your portion in Jesus name.

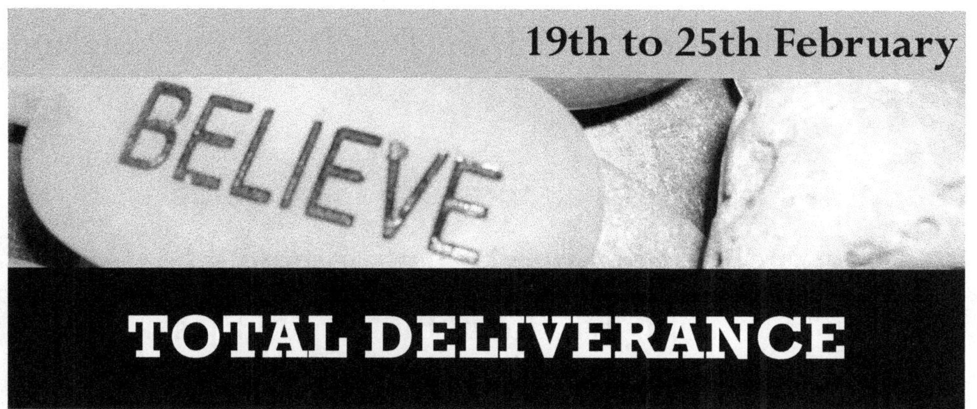

SCRIPTURE FOR THE WEEK

"I am the Lord your God, who brought you out of the land of Egypt, out of the house of bondage." **Exodus 20:2**

CONFESSION

- I believe and confess that my God is my salvation and my deliverer.
- I declare and decree that the gates of brass and bars of iron limiting me are broken in Jesus name.
- I declare that nothing will rob me of my appointment with destiny in the name of Jesus.
- I confess that the pain of the past rejection will no longer hold me down. I reject unforgiveness and bitterness from the past, in the name of Jesus.

- I declare today that I am free from any bondage from the past.
- In this year, I speak to every demonic delay in my life to give way. I decree that nothing will stop my life from being fruitful in the name of Jesus.
- I step into the liberty that Christ has given me. I declare growth and progress in every area of my life.
- Spiritual growth is mine, signs and wonders are my portion. Divine exploits are breaking out in my life in Jesus name.
- I declare today that I am blessed and highly favoured.

PRAYER POINTS FOR THE WEEK

- Command every gates of brass and bars of iron limiting you to be broken in Jesus name.
- Pray in the name of Jesus and destroy anything that wants to rob you of your appointment with destiny.

- In the name of Jesus break the hold of unforgiveness and bitterness from the past over your life.
- Thank God for stepping into the liberty that Christ has given you.

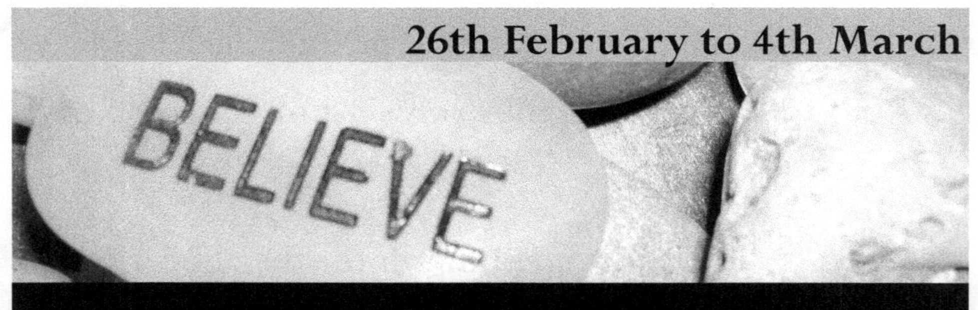

THE MERCIES OF GOD

SCRIPTURE FOR THE WEEK

"Through the Lord's mercies we are not consumed, Because His compassions fail not. They are new every morning; Great is Your faithfulness. "The Lord is my portion," says my soul, "Therefore I hope in Him!"" **Lamentations 3:22-24**

CONFESSION

- I thank the Lord for how far He has brought me and for where He is taking me.
- His mercies has brought us this far and we will finish well in Jesus name.
- I confess today that the mercies of God towards me are new every morning.
- I declare today that I will continue to see the faithfulness of God in my life and I will become a

walking evidence of God's goodness in the lives of men in the name of Jesus.

- As a child of God, I declare today that no matter what comes my way, the Lord is my portion. I have no other options, I have no other alternatives – the Lord is my portion!
- I declare today that I am blessed and highly favoured.

PRAYER POINTS FOR THE WEEK

- Pray in the name of Jesus that the Lord will continue to be your portion.
- Pray in the name of Jesus that you together with your family will become a walking evidence of God's goodness in the lives of men.
- Pray in the name of Jesus that you will continue to see the faithfulness of God in your life.
- Thank God that His mercies towards you are new every morning.

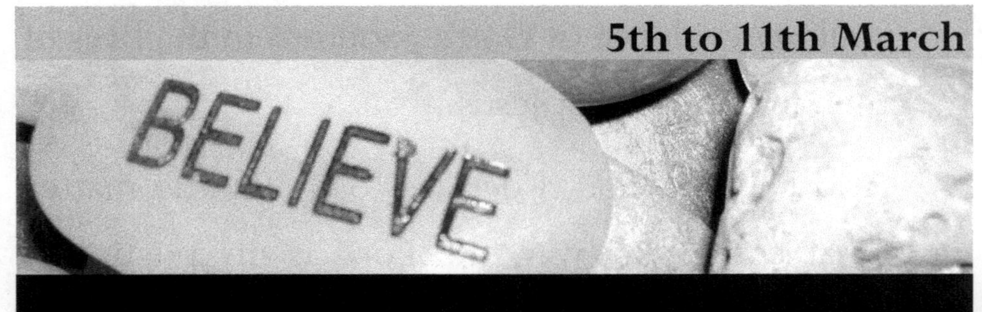

SCRIPTURE FOR THE WEEK

"A Psalm of David. The Lord is my light and my salvation; whom shall I fear? The Lord is the strength of my life; of whom shall I be afraid?" **Psalms 27:1**

CONFESSION

- I believe and confess that the Lord is my light and my salvation.
- I confess that the Lord will be my strength all the days of my life. I declare that fear will not hold me prisoner in any area of my life.
- I decree that from this day, that I will do exploits for God wherever I go.
- I confess that no opposition, no storm or lack will rob me of the opportunity of becoming a living

testimony. I am a walking miracle in the name of Jesus.

- I speak into the week ahead that good news will follow me, harvest will meet harvest in my life and divine manifestation shall be my portion.
- I declare today that I am blessed and highly favoured.

PRAYER POINTS FOR THE WEEK

- Pray in the name of Jesus that the Lord will be your strength all the days of your life.
- Break the hold of fear over your life and declare it will not hold you prisoner in any area of your life.
- Thank God for giving you strength to do exploits for Him wherever you go.
- Thank God that no storm or lack will rob you of the opportunity of becoming a living testimony.

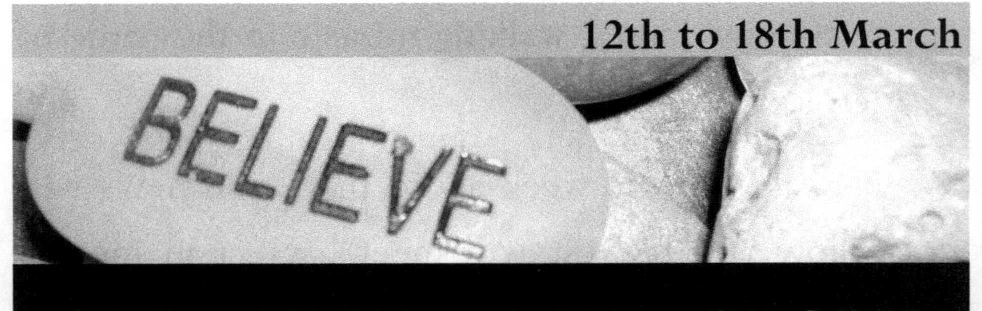

REFLECTING GOD'S GLORY

SCRIPTURE FOR THE WEEK

"Now when they saw the boldness of Peter and John, and perceived that they were uneducated and untrained men, they marveled. And they realized that they had been with Jesus."

Acts 4:13

CONFESSION

- I believe and confess that Jesus Christ is my Lord and Saviour of my life. He is my refuge, my deliverer and the strength of my life.
- I declare today that the glory of God will reflect in every area of my life in the name of Jesus. The Lord will perfect everything concerning me in Jesus name.

- I confess today my life is a walking epistle for the world to read and the world will see good works in my life that glorify God. I declare that every area of my life will yield good works that will be a living testimony of the goodness of God.
- My light will reach many souls for Christ in the name of Jesus. I receive grace and strength to bring souls to Christ. I declare that God will grant me wisdom that will cause me to minister to men and women and see God do great things in their life.
- I confess that I will live to promote the kingdom of God all the days of my life and the goodness of God will never depart from my life. Men will see me and marvel at the goodness of God.
- I declare today that I am blessed and highly favoured.

PRAYER POINTS FOR THE WEEK

- Pray in the name of Jesus, that the Lord will cause His glory to reflect in every area of your life.

- Pray in the name of Jesus that the Lord will make your life a walking epistle for the world to read.
- Pray in the name of Jesus that your life will yield good works that will be a living testimony of the goodness of God.

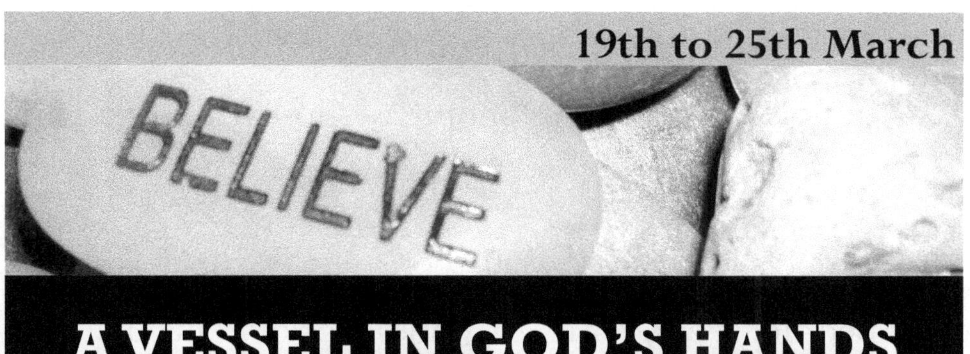

A VESSEL IN GOD'S HANDS

SCRIPTURE FOR THE WEEK

"And let us consider one another in order to stir up love and good works, not forsaking the assembling of ourselves together, as is the manner of some, but exhorting one another, and so much the more as you see the Day approaching."

Hebrews 10:24-25

CONFESSION

- I believe that through the blood of Jesus that was shed for me, I am now a member of the family of God.
- I confess today that as a member of the family of God, nothing shall pluck me out of the hands of my Father. I will continue to be a weapon in the hands of my Father and an obedient child in my walk with Him.

- I declare today that I will be used of God to stir up love amongst the people of God wherever I am planted.
- I declare that I will continually provoke the people around me to good works. Through the grace of God, those who I come into contact with will receive a blessing from my dealings with them, in the name of Jesus.
- I declare today that I will be used of God to serve and encourage others in the house of God.
- I declare today that I am blessed and highly favoured.

PRAYER POINTS FOR THE WEEK

- Pray in the name of Jesus that as a member of the family of God, nothing shall pluck you out of the hands of your Father.
- Ask the Lord to use you to stir up love amongst the people of God wherever you are planted.
- Pray in the name of Jesus for the grace to continually provoke the people around you to

good works.

- Thank the Lord that you will be used of God to serve and encourage others in the house of God.

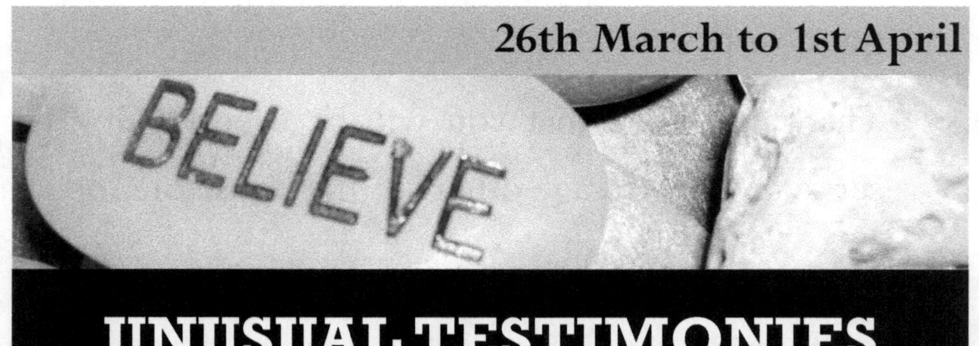

SCRIPTURE FOR THE WEEK

"Come and hear, all you who fear God, and I will declare what He has done for my soul." **Psalms 66:16**

CONFESSION

- I believe and confess that I have entered a season of great manifestations in the name of Jesus.
- I declare and decree that this month will deliver unusual testimonies into my life. I will give testimonies that no man can claim credit for. I will give testimonies that will beat the understanding of the experts.
- I decree that great grace and great favour will manifest in every area of my life. I will walk into blessings that exceed my own expectation.

- From this day onwards, God will make me a walking example of His favour in the affairs of men. I am a walking testimony. I am the evidence of the grace and mercy of God.
- From this day, new songs of celebration will break out in my life. The sound of joyous celebration is my portion in the name of Jesus. My story is changing from glory to glory!
- I declare today that I am blessed and highly favoured.

PRAYER POINTS FOR THE WEEK

- Thank the Lord for ushering you into a season of great manifestations in the name of Jesus.
- Pray in the name of Jesus that this week will deliver unusual testimonies into your life.
- Pray in the name of Jesus that from this day onwards, God will make you a walking example of His favour in the affairs of men.
- Thank God for changing your story from glory to glory and causing joyous celebration to be your portion in the name of Jesus.

SCRIPTURE FOR THE WEEK

"Surely goodness and mercy shall follow me All the days of my life; And I will dwell in the house of the Lord Forever." **Psalms 23:6**

CONFESSION

- I believe and confess that the Lord God is my strength and my salvation. I declare that because of the death of Christ at the cross at Calvary, my victory is established.
- I confess today that the grace and mercies of God that has brought me to the house of God will keep me firmly planted.
- I declare that no delay, storm or distraction will keep me away from the house of the Lord. I

confess that the word of God in His house will cause me to walk in great blessing.

- I will not miss any blessing that is due me in the name of Jesus. I declare that nothing shall rob me of what God has destined for me.
- I confess today that I will dwell in the house of the Lord all the days of my life and so will my children and my children's children. The zeal for your house shall never depart from my family in the name of Jesus.
- I declare today that I am blessed and highly favoured.

PRAYER POINTS FOR THE WEEK

- Pray in the name of Jesus that the grace and mercies of God that has brought you to the house of God will keep you firmly planted.
- Pray in the name of Jesus that no delay, storm or distraction will keep you away from the house of the Lord.

- Pray in the name of Jesus that you will not miss any blessing that is due as you remain planted in the house of God.
- Thank God that as you dwell in the house of the Lord all the days of your life, so shall it be with your children and your children's children.

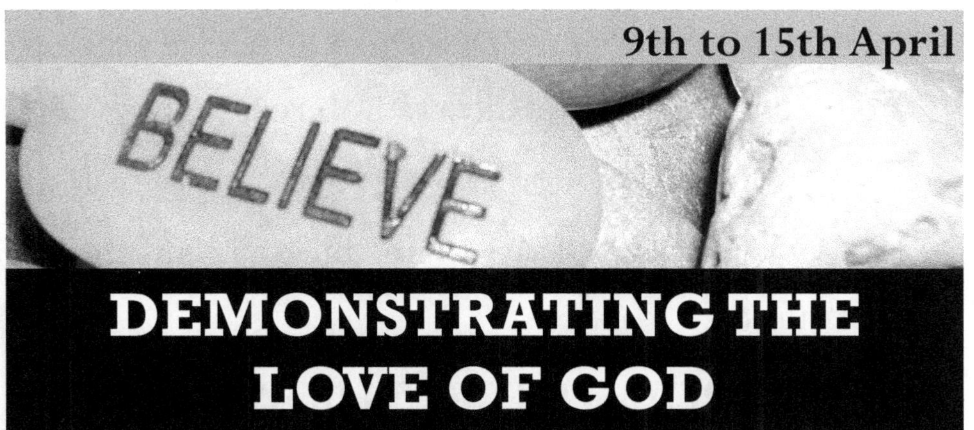

9th to 15th April

DEMONSTRATING THE LOVE OF GOD

SCRIPTURE FOR THE WEEK

"This is my commandment: Love each other in the same way I have loved you." **John 15:12**

CONFESSION

- I believe and confess that I serve a Living God who sacrificed His only Son for my salvation.
- I confess that from today, I will walk in love towards everyone that I meet.
- I declare that the love of God is shed abroad in my heart from this day onwards and the fruits of that divine love will be seen in every area of my life.
- I believe and confess that all my relationships will reflect the love of God and people will see God's glory in my relationships.

- Today, I receive grace to forgive. I receive grace to be kind and tender-hearted. I receive grace to love even difficult people.
- I declare today that I am blessed and highly favoured.

PRAYER POINTS FOR THE WEEK

- Ask the Lord to help you walk in love towards everyone that you meet today in Jesus name.
- Pray in the name of Jesus that the love of God will be shed abroad in your heart from this day onwards.
- Pray in the name of Jesus that the fruits of that divine love will be seen in every area of your life.
- Thank God for the grace to forgive, grace to be kind and tender-hearted, grace to love even difficult people.

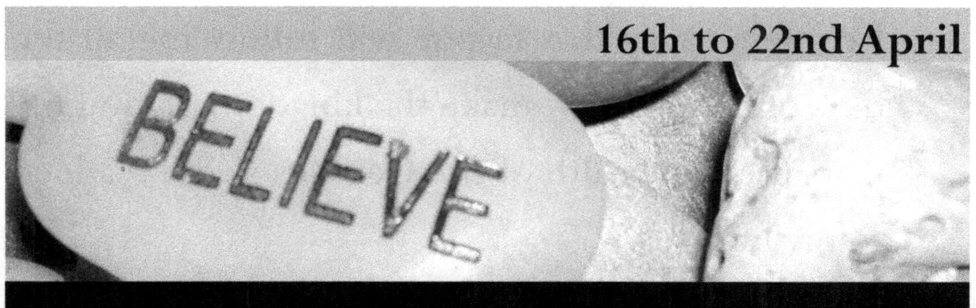

SCRIPTURE OF THE WEEK

" Therefore your gates shall be open continually; They shall not be shut day or night, That men may bring to you the wealth of the Gentiles, And their kings in procession." **Isaiah 60:11**

CONFESSION

- I believe and confess that I have entered a season of uncommon favour.
- I declare and decree that anything resisting my blessing is removed in the name of Jesus.
- As a child of God, I decree that agents of favour are coming into my life from the north, south, east and west.

- I confess today that favour will follow me all the days of my life. As I make the kingdom of God my priority, the wealth of the Gentiles shall be added to my life.
- From today, the blessing of the Lord will rest upon the work of my hands and I will be a living example of God's favour here on earth.
- I declare today that I am blessed and highly favoured.

PRAYER POINTS FOR THE WEEK

- In the name of Jesus command anything resisting your blessing to be removed.
- Pray in the name of Jesus that agents of favour will come into your life from the north, south, east and west.
- Pray in the name of Jesus that favour will follow you all the days of your life and as you make the kingdom of God your priority, the wealth of the Gentiles shall be added to your life.

- Thank God that from today, the blessing of the Lord will rest upon the work of your hands and you will be a living example of God's favour here on earth.

23rd to 29th April

GODLINESS

SCRIPTURE OF THE WEEK

"Have nothing to do with godless myths and old wives' tales; rather, train yourself to be godly. For physical training is of some value, but godliness has value for all things, holding promise for both the present life and the life to come." **1 Timothy 4:7-8**

CONFESSION

- I believe and confess that God the Father sent His Son to come and die for me. I declare that through this sacrifice I am reconciled to God.

- As a child of God, I decree that the power that raised Jesus from the dead will reign in my daily life. I will have victory in every area of my life in the name of Jesus.

- I confess today that I break the hold of unhelpful traditions making God's word ineffective in my life.
- I confess that I will not just know about my God but I will know Him for myself. My passion for God will grow stronger and stronger in the name of Jesus.
- I declare that by the blood of Jesus, I am dead to sin and alive to the things of God. I declare that my spirit is responsive to what God has for me in the name of Jesus.
- I confess today that I break free from anything that is holding back my spiritual growth in the name of Jesus. I am free from guilt, I am free from discouragement, I am free from bitterness and I am free from every bondage in the name of Jesus.
- I declare today that I am blessed and highly favoured.

PRAYER POINTS FOR THE WEEK

- Pray in the name of Jesus that the power that raised Jesus from the dead will reign in your daily life.
- Break the hold of any unhelpful traditions that is making God's word ineffective in your life.
- Break free from anything that is holding back your spiritual growth in the name of Jesus.
- Pray that you will have victory in both your private and public life in the name of Jesus.

BREAKING FREE FROM FEAR

SCRIPTURE FOR THE WEEK

"The Lord is my light and my salvation; whom shall I fear? The Lord is the strength of my life; of whom shall I be afraid? When the wicked came against me to eat up my flesh, my enemies and foes, they stumbled and fell." **Psalms 27:1-2**

CONFESSION

- I believe and confess that the Lord is my light and my salvation.
- I declare based on His word that the walls of fear have fallen off every area of my life.
- I declare that from today, I will not be a prisoner to fear in my life. I confess that my faith destroys any attack of fear in the name of Jesus. I refuse to yield to fear in any endeavour of my life.

- I confess that any situation trying to intimidate me will lead to my elevation in the name of Jesus.
- I declare that any situation trying to intimidate me will usher me into great harvest in the name of Jesus.
- I declare that any situation trying to intimidate me will bring me into my destined place in the name of Jesus.
- I declare today that I am blessed and highly favoured.

PRAYER POINTS FOR THE WEEK

- In the name of Jesus, command the walls of fear to fall off every area of your life.
- Pray in the name of Jesus that you will not be a prisoner to fear in your life.
- Pray in the name of Jesus that your faith will destroy any attack of fear.
- Thank God that any situation trying to intimidate you will bring you into you destined place in the name of Jesus.

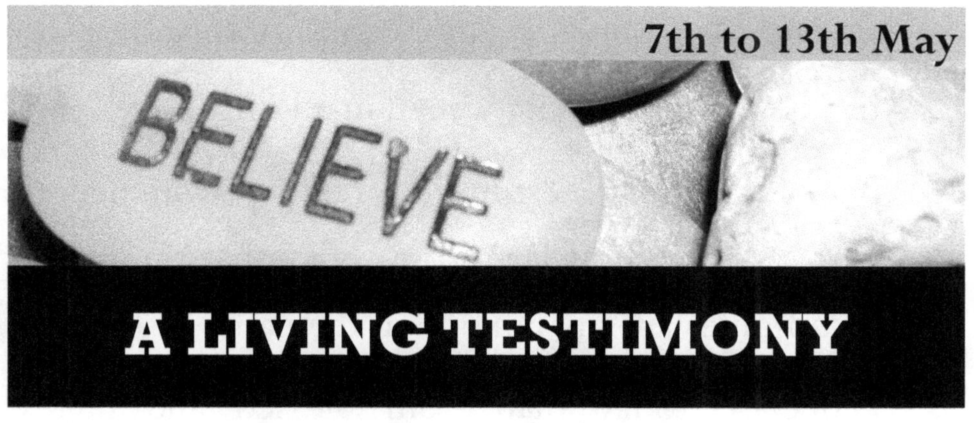

SCRIPTURE FOR THE WEEK

"For all things are for your sakes, that grace, having spread through the many, may cause thanksgiving to abound to the glory of God." **2 Corinthians 4:15**

CONFESSION

- I believe and confess that I am created to reflect the glory of God.
- I declare and decree that everything about my life will reflect the glory of God.
- Anything that will bring shame to my life is removed in the name of Jesus. Anything meant to tarnish my testimony is removed right now, in the name of Jesus.

- I confess today that I will excel in the work of my hands. I will be distinguished in all I do.
- I am a walking testimony and the evidence of God's favour. I declare from today that significant testimonies are my portion in the name of Jesus.
- I declare today that I am blessed and highly favoured.

PRAYER POINTS FOR THE WEEK

- Pray in the name of Jesus that everything about your life will reflect the glory of God.
- In the name of Jesus command anything that will bring shame to your life to be removed.
- In the name of Jesus destroy anything meant to tarnish your testimony.
- Thank the Lord that from today significant testimonies are your portions in the name of Jesus.

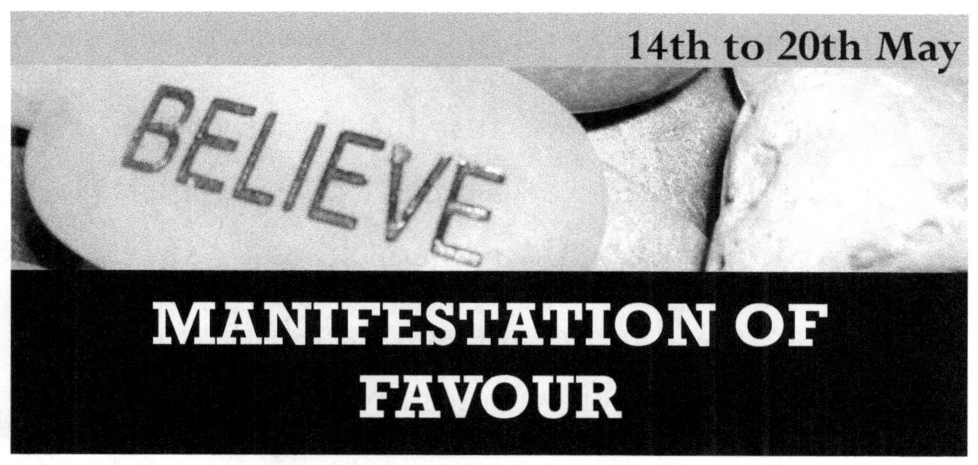

MANIFESTATION OF FAVOUR

SCRIPTURE FOR THE WEEK

"A good man obtains favor from the Lord, but a man of wicked intentions He will condemn." **Proverbs 12:2**

CONFESSION

- I declare that in this month, the wisdom of God will release many solutions in my life in the name of Jesus.
- The doors that have refused to open to me will be opened by the Hand of God.
- I confess today that I will pursue the wisdom of God with all my might, all my strength and all my mind.
- I declare today that as I continue to seek the face of God, favour will break out in every area of my

life in the name of Jesus.

- I believe and confess that the favour of God will follow me wherever I go. I will encounter good news this week in the name of Jesus.
- Blessings will follow me and overshadow me and I will end this week with testimonies in Jesus name.
- I declare today that I am blessed and highly favoured.

PRAYER POINTS FOR THE WEEK

- Ask the Lord for the wisdom of God that will release many solutions in your life in the name of Jesus.
- Pray in the name of Jesus for the grace to pursue the wisdom of God with all your might, all your strength and all your mind.
- Pray in the name of Jesus that as you continue to seek the face of God, favour will break out in every area of your life.
- Thank God that His blessings will follow you and overshadow you as you become a source of solutions for impossible situation.

PLEASING GOD

SCRIPTURE FOR THE WEEK

" By faith Enoch was taken away so that he did not see death, "and was not found, because God had taken him"; for before he was taken he had this testimony, that he pleased God."

Hebrews 11:5

CONFESSION

- I believe and confess that I am created for a purpose and that purpose will be fulfilled.
- I confess that from today every area of my life will please God. I decree that after all is said and done, my testimony will be that I pleased God.
- I declare that God is writing a new chapter of my life. My prayer life will provoke divine results in my life.

- Unusual breakthroughs are released into my present and future life in the name of Jesus.
- I speak into the week ahead that doors of great favour will open to me. I declare that God will bring completion to long-running battles in my life in the name of Jesus.
- I declare today that I am blessed and highly favoured.

PRAYER POINTS FOR THE WEEK

- Pray in the name of Jesus for the grace to fulfil the purpose for which you were created.
- Pray in the name of Jesus that from today every area of your life will please God.
- Pray in the name of Jesus that unusual breakthroughs will be released into your present and future life as you seek to please God.
- Thank the Lord that after all is said and done, your testimony will be that you pleased God.

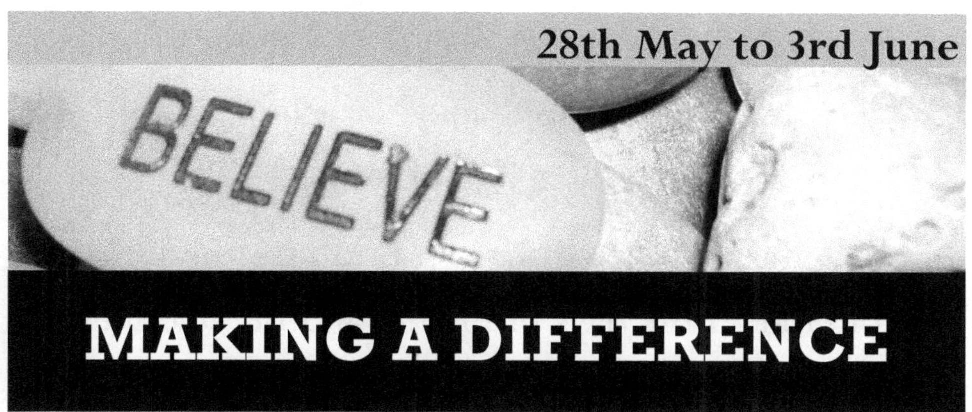

SCRIPTURE FOR THE WEEK

"In Him was life, and the life was the light of men. And the light shines in the darkness, and the darkness did not comprehend it." **John 1:4-5**

CONFESSION

- I believe and confess that Jesus Christ is the true Light and the light of men. He has declared me as the light of the world and I dedicate my life to that cause.
- I declare today that all the days of my life, I will reflect this light and no darkness can withstand my light.
- I confess today that any evil cloud of darkness encroaching in any area of my life is removed right now in the name of Jesus.

- I declare that everywhere I go, I will be a voice for Jesus. I refuse to yield to the pressure to compromise in the name of Jesus.
- I confess that I will live to promote the kingdom of God all the days of my life and the goodness of God will never depart from my life.
- I declare today that I am blessed and highly favoured.

PRAYER POINTS FOR THE WEEK

- Jesus has declared you as the light of the world; ask for grace to dedicate your life to that cause.
- Pray in the name of Jesus that all the days of your life, you will reflect this light and no darkness can withstand your light.
- In the name of Jesus, command any evil cloud of darkness encroaching in any area of your life to be removed right now.
- Thank God that you will live to promote the kingdom of God all the days of your life and the goodness of God will never depart from your life.

SCRIPTURE FOR THE WEEK

"Be anxious for nothing, but in everything by prayer and supplication, with thanksgiving, let your requests be made known to God; and the peace of God, which surpasses all understanding, will guard your hearts and minds through Christ Jesus." **Philippians 4:6-7**

CONFESSION

- I believe and confess that my God is Almighty and He has brought me into His family through the blood of Christ.
- I declare that as a child of God, my prayer will be heard in the house of the Lord throughout my life. I confess that prayer shall be my lifestyle in the name of the Jesus.

- As a member of this great family of God, I refuse to be a victim of anxiety.
- Instead of persistent complaints and despair, my mouth will be filled with thanksgiving and praise.
- I believe and confess that my prayer of faith will trigger unusual peace over my life. I will grow from strength to strength and from glory to glory as my heart and mind is secured by the peace of God.
- I confess even in raging violent storms, the unusual peace of God will sustain me and I will come out victorious.
- I declare today that I am blessed and highly favoured.

PRAYER POINTS FOR THE WEEK

- Pray in the name of Jesus for the grace to make prayer your lifestyle.
- Pray in the name of Jesus that your desire for the word of God will never wane.

- Pray in the name of Jesus that as you walk in line with the word of God, you will grow from strength to strength and from glory to glory.
- Thank the Lord that the word of God will continue to be your sword of the spirit.

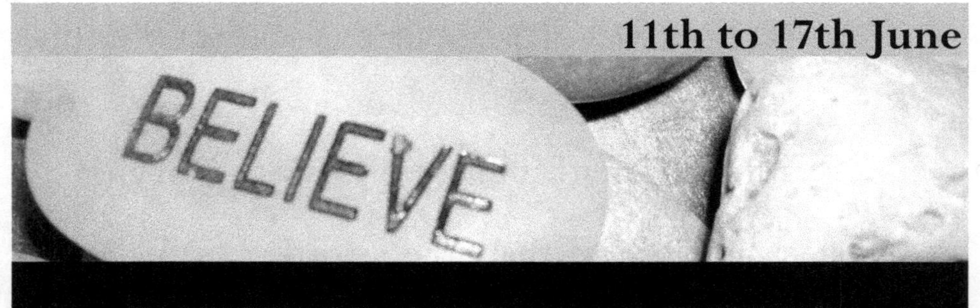

SCRIPTURE FOR THE WEEK

"When a man's ways please the Lord, He makes even his enemies to be at peace with him." **Proverbs 16:7**

CONFESSION

- I believe and confess that in this week, unusual testimonies will follow me wherever I go.
- I declare and decree that even those who have conspired against me will begin working in my favour in the name of Jesus.
- I declare today that good news will come from far and near into my life. Good news will meet good news in my life.
- As I walk in obedience to God's word, His blessings will manifest in every area of my life.

- Those who are set against me are about to admit that the hand of God is at work in my life.
- I believe and confess that God has made me a walking testimony. My life will attract blessing and favour that will baffle my critics. God is about to cause even my enemies to usher me into my breakthrough.
- I declare today that I am blessed and highly favoured.

PRAYER POINTS FOR THE WEEK

- Pray in the name of Jesus that from today unusual testimonies will follow you wherever you go.
- Pray in the name of Jesus that even those who have conspired against you will begin working in you favour.
- Pray in the name of Jesus that as you walk in obedience to God's word, His blessings will manifest in every area of your life.
- Thank God for making you a walking testimony.

SCRIPTURE FOR THE WEEK

"Those who are planted in the house of the Lord Shall flourish in the courts of our God." **Psalms 92:13**

CONFESSION

- I believe and confess that the blessing of the Lord rests upon my life.
- I declare that as I remain planted in the house of the Lord, I will continue to flourish on every side.
- I confess today that fruitfulness will manifest in everything that I do in the name of Jesus.
- I declare that from today, success will attend everything that I set myself to do in the name of Jesus.

- I will experience success even in the desert places.
- I will experience the manifestation that men consider impossible, in the name of Jesus.
- Doors that have remained closed for years will begin opening up to me now, in the name of Jesus.
- I confess today that I receive unusual blessing and breakthroughs in the name of Jesus.
- I receive wealth and riches in my life, in the name of Jesus.
- I receive divine elevation in the name of Jesus.
- From today, God will cause my name to be mentioned in the right places and by the right people in the name of Jesus.
- Agents of favour are coming into my life from North, South, East and the West in the name of Jesus.
- I declare today that I am blessed and highly favoured.

PRAYER POINTS FOR THE WEEK

- Pray in the name of Jesus that the blessing of the Lord will rest upon your life.
- Pray in the name of Jesus that you will continue to flourish on every side as you remain planted in the house of the Lord.
- Pray in the name of Jesus that from today fruitfulness will manifest in everything that you do.
- Thank the Lord that you will experience success even in the desert places.

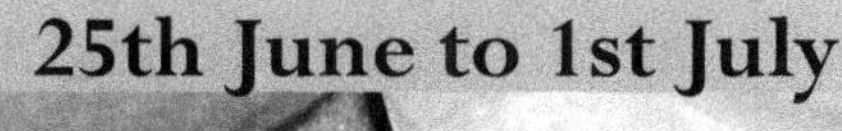

OVERCOMING IMPOSSIBLE SITUATIONS

SCRIPTURE FOR THE WEEK

"Jesus said to him, "If you can believe, all things are possible to him who believes."" **Mark 9:23**

CONFESSION

- I believe and confess that my God is a miracle worker.
- He makes a way in the wilderness and causes rivers to break out even in the desert.
- I declare today that I am coming out of every tight situation with a major testimony. Every major problem I am facing will result in a major testimony in Jesus name.
- I decree today that no God-given tool in my hand will be lost in battle. I speak restoration to every

area of my life right now. I declare that the life of God will restore any area of my life that has become unfruitful.

- I confess that major doors will open to me in the name of Jesus. I am walking into major miracles right now in the name of Jesus.
- I will be the subject of testimonies that will defy logic in the name of Jesus.
- I declare today that I am blessed and highly favoured.

PRAYER POINTS FOR THE WEEK

- Pray in the name of Jesus that you will come out of every tight situation with a major testimony.
- Pray in the name of Jesus that every major problem you are facing will result in a major testimony.
- Pray in the name of Jesus that no God-given tool in your hand will be lost in battle.
- Pray in the name of Jesus that major doors will open to you out of every tight situation.

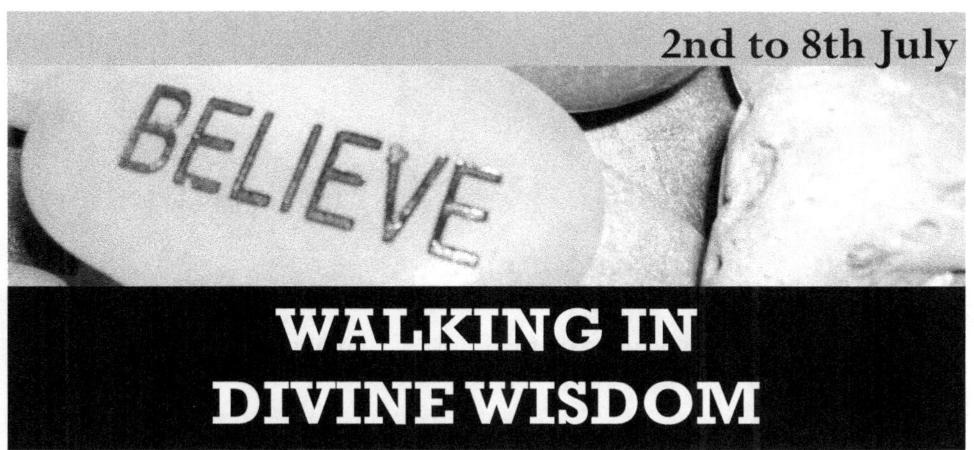

WALKING IN DIVINE WISDOM

SCRIPTURE FOR THE WEEK

"Wisdom will multiply your days and add years to your life. If you become wise, you will be the one to benefit. If you scorn wisdom, you will be the one to suffer." **Proverbs 9:11-12**

CONFESSION

- I believe and confess that I serve the One who knows the end from the beginning. His wisdom surpasses all.
- I declare today that I'll seek His wisdom concerning every area of my life. The Lord will order my steps as I walk in wisdom. I will not fall victim to deception in the name of Jesus.
- I confess that the Lord will open my eyes and I will not operate in ignorance or in darkness. May every

hidden evil trap be exposed in the name of Jesus.

- I receive divine promotion in every area of my life as I exalt wisdom. I declare that the Lord will beautify my life with honour.
- I declare today that I am blessed and highly favoured.

PRAYER POINTS FOR THE WEEK

- Pray in the name Jesus that from today you will seek His wisdom concerning every area of your life.
- Pray in the name Jesus that from today the Lord will order your steps as you walk in wisdom.
- Pray in the name Jesus that you will not fall victim to deception.
- Pray in the name Jesus that every hidden evil trap be exposed as the Lord opens your eyes.

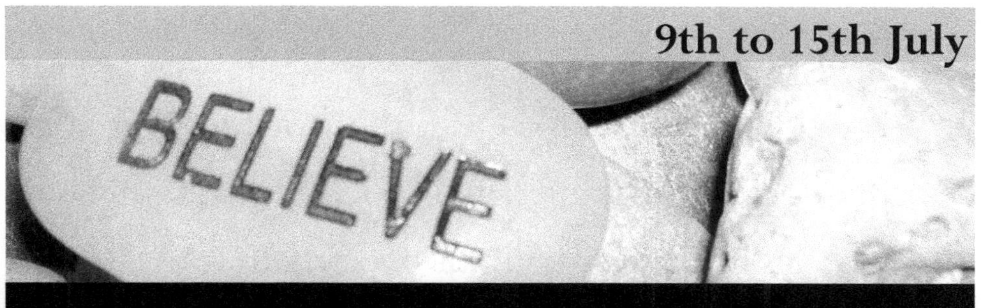

LORD, DIRECT MY STEPS

SCRIPTURE FOR THE WEEK

"Direct my steps by Your word, And let no iniquity have dominion over me. Redeem me from the oppression of man, that I may keep Your precepts." **Psalms 119:133-134**

CONFESSION

- I believe and confess that God has perfect plans for my life. I declare today that my steps are ordered by the Lord and that I will not fall in the trap of the enemy.
- I confess that God has granted me wisdom and boldness to make choices that will glorify Him all the days of my life.
- I declare that I will not yield to the pressures of society. I will not labour under the oppression of

people.

- I declare that I will keep to the word of God in all my decision-making. I will operate in the light of God and darkness will not overwhelm me.
- I decree that I will not fall victim to the trap of the devil or evil men. Every snare laid on my path shall be destroyed before I get there in the name of Jesus.
- I declare today that I am blessed and highly favoured.

PRAYER POINTS FOR THE WEEK

- Pray in the name of Jesus that your steps will continually be ordered by the Lord and that you will not fall in the trap of the enemy.
- Pray in the name of Jesus that God will grant you wisdom and boldness to make choices that will glorify Him all the days of your life.
- Pray in the name of Jesus that no matter what comes your way you will not yield to the pressures of society.

- Pray in the name of Jesus that you will keep to the word of God in all your decision-making.

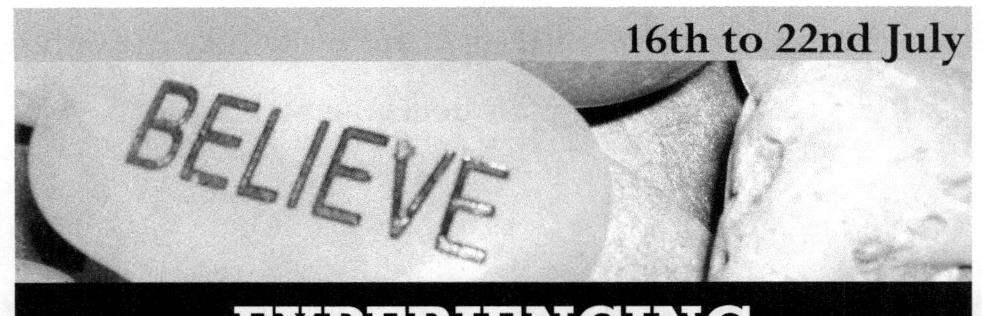

16th to 22nd July

EXPERIENCING GOD'S PROMISES

SCRIPTURE FOR THE WEEK

"But as it is written, Eye hath not seen, nor ear heard, neither have entered into the heart of man, the things which God hath prepared for them that love him."
1 Corinthians 2:9

CONFESSION

- I believe and confess that I have entered a season of uncommon favour.
- I declare and decree that unusual testimonies are breaking out in my life in the name of Jesus.
- As a child of God, I refuse to be average and have average experience in God.
- I confess today that my spiritual life will experience growth that I have never seen before.

Signs and wonders are breaking out in my life in the name of Jesus.

- Great grace is coming upon me right now. Uncommon favour is following me wherever I go.
- From today, I declare that what God has said concerning me will be my experience. My expectation will not be cut off in the name of Jesus.
- I declare today that I am blessed and highly favoured.

PRAYER POINTS FOR THE WEEK

- Pray in the name of Jesus that unusual testimonies will break out in your life.
- Pray in the name of Jesus that your spiritual life will experience growth that you have never seen before.
- Pray in the name of Jesus that from today, what God has said concerning you will be your experience.
- Thank God that your expectation will not be cut off in the name of Jesus.

SCRIPTURE FOR THE WEEK

" For sin shall not have dominion over you, for you are not under law but under grace." **Romans 6:14**

CONFESSION

- I believe and confess that the Lord Jesus died for me and paid the ultimate price for my sins.
- I confess today that Jesus came to take away my sins and my righteousness is now in God.
- I declare and decree that as a true child of God, sin will not have dominion over me in the name of Jesus. By the grace of God, I will overcome every temptation and trial that will come my way.
- I declare that by the grace of God, I will live a life of humility and a life totally committed to the

obedience of Christ throughout my life.

- I believe and confess that as I continue in humility and obedience, the Lord will elevate me in the name of Jesus. God will cause me to ride in high places and the devil will remain under my feet continuously.
- I declare today that I am blessed and highly favoured.

PRAYER POINTS FOR THE WEEK

- Pray in the name of Jesus that as a true child of God, sin will not have dominion over you.
- Pray in the name of Jesus for the grace to overcome every temptation and trial that will come your way.
- Pray in the name of Jesus that God will continuously cause you to ride in high places and the devil will remain under your feet.
- Thank the Lord that as you continue in humility and obedience, the Lord will elevate you in the name of Jesus.

30th July to 5th August

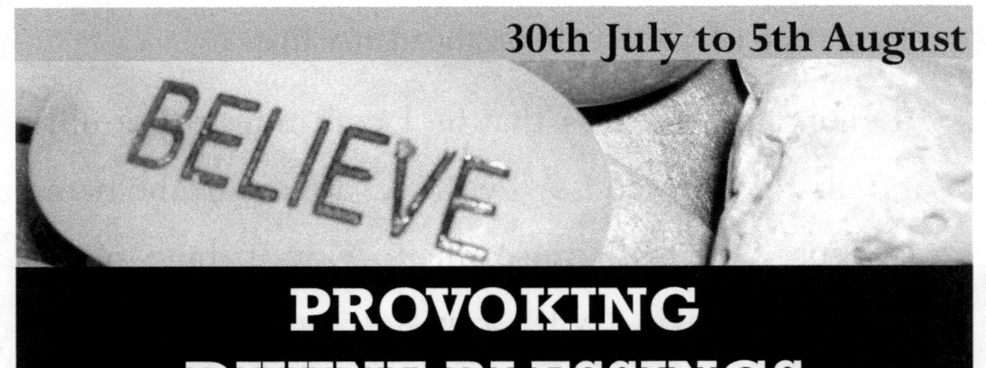

PROVOKING DIVINE BLESSINGS

SCRIPTURE FOR THE WEEK

" Bring all the tithes into the storehouse, That there may be food in My house, And try Me now in this," Says the Lord of hosts, "If I will not open for you the windows of heaven And pour out for you such blessing That there will not be room enough to receive it." **Malachi 3:10**

CONFESSION

- I believe and confess that the God I serve is a great and faithful God. Every word that comes out of His mouth shall be fulfilled in my life in Jesus name.
- I confess today that as I bring my tithes and offerings to the house of God, I provoke divine blessing upon my life. I declare today that I am

walking in unusual blessing and confess that I will receive blessing that will exceed my storehouse.

- Every devourer set against me shall fail. Every leakage in my finances is stopped in Jesus name.
- I confess today that the blessing of the Lord rests upon the work of my hands. Success shall attend everything I put my hand to. As I am directed by God, everything I set out to do shall be fruitful in Jesus name.
- I declare that I will be a committed kingdom promoter for the rest of my life. People will come to know the Lord Jesus because of my investment in the kingdom of God.
- I declare today that I am blessed and highly favoured.

PRAYER POINTS FOR THE WEEK

- Pray in the name of Jesus that every word that comes out of His mouth shall be fulfilled in your life.

- Pray in the name of Jesus that as you bring your tithes and offerings to the house of God, you provoke divine blessing upon your life.
- Pray in the name of Jesus that every devourer set against you shall fail and every leakage in your finances be stopped right now.
- Pray in the name of Jesus that the blessing of the Lord will rest upon the work of your hands.

SCRIPTURE FOR THE WEEK

"And now, Israel, what does the Lord your God require of you, but to fear the Lord your God, to walk in all His ways and to love Him, to serve the Lord your God with all your heart and with all your soul." **Deuteronomy 10:12**

CONFESSION

- I believe and confess that I am created to honour God with every part of my life.
- I declare and decree that from today, God's praises will continually fill my mouth. I choose to glorify God in all circumstances.
- I declare that every storm or challenge meant to steal the joy of the Lord from my life will fail. I replace complaints and murmuring with praise and worship.

- I confess today that I will go all out to honour God in my life. I will honour Him in my spiritual life, I will honour Him in my family life, I will honour Him in my business and career life. I will honour him with my strength, my talents and my resources.
- I confess that God will lift me and establish me in high places as I continue to honour him.
- I declare today that I am blessed and highly favoured.

PRAYER POINTS FOR THE WEEK

- Pray in the name of Jesus that all the days of your life, you will be someone who honours God with every part of your life.
- Pray in the name of Jesus that every storm or challenge meant to steal the joy of the Lord from your life will fail.
- Pray in the name of Jesus for the grace to honour God in your spiritual life, your family life, business and career life.

- Thank God that He will lift you and establish you in high places as you continue to honour him.

SCRIPTURE FOR THE WEEK

"Is anything too hard for the Lord? At the appointed time I will return to you, according to the time of life, and Sarah shall have a son." **Genesis 18:14**

CONFESSION

- I believe and confess that I serve a great God and there is nothing too hard for Him.
- I declare and decree that there is no miracle or testimony that is beyond my reach.
- Today, I reject doubt and fear from my mind. I declare that their hold over me is broken in Jesus name.
- I confess that I am laying hold of signs and wonders in my life right now. I declare and decree

that people will marvel when they hear what God has done in my life today.

- I declare today that God is sending His agents of favour into my life right now. I have received testimonies that will only give glory to God.
- Healing is mine, divine health is my portion in the name of Jesus. My story is about to baffle the experts this year.
- I declare today that I am blessed and highly favoured.

PRAYER POINTS FOR THE WEEK

- Thank the Lord that there is no miracle or testimony that is beyond your reach.
- Command the hold of fear and doubt to be broken over your life.
- Pray in the name of Jesus that no fear or doubt will prevent you from laying hold of signs and wonders in your life.
- Thank the Lord that your story is about to baffle the experts this year in Jesus name.

20th to 26th August

THE BLESSING OF FRUITFULNESS

SCRIPTURE FOR THE WEEK

"'For I will look on you favorably and make you fruitful, multiply you and confirm My covenant with you. You shall eat the old harvest, and clear out the old because of the new."
Leviticus 26:9-10

CONFESSION

- In this month, I declare that the favour of God will not pass me by.
- The heavens over my life are open and I receive the blessing of fruitfulness and multiplication in my life in the name of Jesus.
- I confess today that the work of my hands shall be blessed beyond measure and I will experience abundance on every side in the name of Jesus.

- I declare today that unusual harvest will break out in my life in the name of Jesus.
- I believe and confess that the favour of God will unleash abundance that will exceed my storehouses in the name of Jesus. I declare that harvest will meet harvest in my life in Jesus name.
- I declare today that I am blessed and highly favoured.

PRAYER POINTS FOR THE WEEK

- Pray in the name of Jesus that the heavens over your life will be opened to receive the blessing of fruitfulness and multiplication.
- Pray in the name of Jesus that from today the work of your hands shall be blessed beyond measure.
- Pray in the name of Jesus that you will experience abundance on every side.
- Thank the Lord for the favour of God will unleash abundance that will exceed your storehouses in the name of Jesus.

SCRIPTURE FOR THE WEEK

"I have been crucified with Christ; it is no longer I who live, but Christ lives in me; and the life which I now live in the flesh I live by faith in the Son of God, who loved me and gave Himself for me." **Galatians 2:20**

CONFESSION

- I believe and confess that Jesus Christ paid the ultimate price for my life. I confess that by the grace of God I am living a new life for Christ.
- I declare that the resurrection power of Christ is manifesting in every area of my life.
- I decree today that anything that the devil has stolen is restored today in the name of Jesus.
- I decree that anything that the devil has killed in my life is resurrecting right now in the name of

Jesus.

- I speak into the week ahead that the things that experts have given up on concerning my life will experience a turnaround in the name of Jesus.
- I am walking in power for a new life. I am a new creature in Christ Jesus.
- I declare today that I am blessed and highly favoured.

PRAYER POINTS FOR THE WEEK

- Pray in the name of Jesus that the resurrection power of Christ will manifest in every area of your life.
- Pray in the name of Jesus that anything that the devil has stolen be restored today.
- Pray in the name of Jesus that the things that experts have given up on concerning your life will experience a turnaround.
- Thank God that you are walking in power for a new life because you are new creature in Christ Jesus.

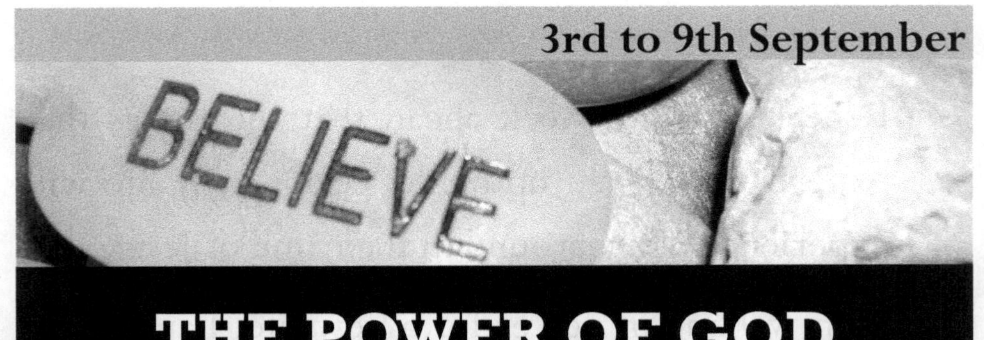

SCRIPTURE FOR THE WEEK

"For I am not ashamed of the gospel of Christ, for it is the power of God to salvation for everyone who believes, for the Jew first and also for the Greek. For in it the righteousness of God is revealed from faith to faith; as it is written, "The just shall live by faith.""

Romans 1:16-17

CONFESSION

- I believe and confess that Jesus Christ is the Lord and Saviour of my life and the power of God has been made available to me through this gospel.
- I declare today that by the power of God any attempt of the devil to delay my testimony will fail. I declare an immediate end to any demonic delays in the name of Jesus.

- I refuse to hide my witness for Christ wherever I go. I declare that all the days of my life, I will live for Christ.
- May everyone who comes into contact with me see the glory of the Lord upon my life. May I carry God's presence and favour wherever I go, in Jesus name.
- I declare that I will manifest the power of God in a world of compromise. The power of God will cause me to excel in all that I put my hand to, in the name of Jesus. My life will bear fruit that will bring glory to God alone.
- I declare today that I am blessed and highly favoured.

PRAYER POINTS FOR THE WEEK

- Thank the Lord that the power of God has been made available to you through this gospel.
- Pray in the name of Jesus that by the power of God any attempt of the devil to delay your testimony will fail.

- Pray in the name of Jesus for the boldness not to hide your witness for Christ wherever you go.
- Pray in the name of Jesus that all the days of your life, you will live for Christ unashamed.

LOVING THE MOST HIGH GOD

SCRIPTURE FOR THE WEEK

"And you shall love the Lord your God with all your heart, with all your soul, with all your mind, and with all your strength.' This is the first commandment." **Mark 12:30**

CONFESSION

- I believe and confess that I am a child of God, because of the blood of Christ. I am in the kingdom of the God and Jesus is still my Lord.
- I declare today that from this day onwards, I will serve the Lord with all gifts, talents and abilities. I declare that I will use what God has given me for the advancement of His kingdom in the name of Jesus.
- As a member of this great kingdom, I confess that

I am a co-labourer with Christ in His vineyard. By the grace of God, I will lead souls to Christ. I confess that God will use me to turn many to Himself, in the name of Jesus.

- I confess today that I walk into a harvest of souls for Christ, in the name of Jesus.
- As a child of God, I declare that the grace of God will abound towards me and that wealth and riches will be in my house.
- I believe and confess that I will be a promoter of the kingdom of God. The blessing and protection of God will continue to rest upon my life and all that pertains to me, in Jesus name.
- I declare today that I am blessed and highly favoured.

PRAYER POINTS FOR THE WEEK

- Pray in the name of Jesus that from today onwards, you will serve the Lord with all your gifts, talents and abilities.

- Pray in the name of Jesus for the grace to use what God has given you for the advancement of His kingdom.
- Pray in the name of Jesus that the Lord will use you to turn many to Himself.
- Pray in the name of Jesus that the blessing and protection of God will continue to rest upon your life and all that pertains to you as you promote the Kingdom of God.

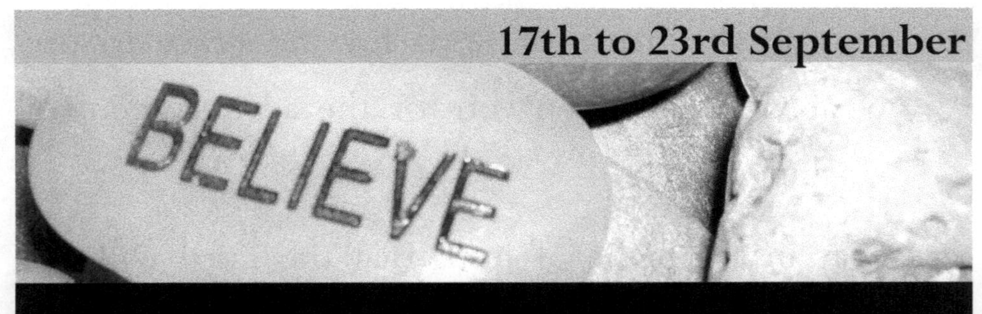

LORD, HAVE YOUR WAY

SCRIPTURE FOR THE WEEK

"The Lord said to me, "You have seen correctly, for I am watching to see that my word is fulfilled."" **Jeremiah 1:12**

CONFESSION

- I believe and confess that in this month, I will testify of the goodness of God in my life.
- I declare that I will walk into great and significant testimonies that will be beyond the understanding of men.
- No matter what the devil says, God will have His way in my life.
- I declare today that no storm, no drought or dark seasons will cause me to lose focus of God's word concerning my life.
- I am in a season of mighty manifestations and God

has made me a walking testimony in every area of my life.

- God is making me a blessing to my generation. God is fulfilling every word that He has spoken concerning me.
- Nothing will stop what God is set to do in my life, in the name of Jesus.
- I declare today that I am blessed and highly favoured.

PRAYER POINTS FOR THE WEEK

- Pray in the name of Jesus that you will walk into great and significant testimonies that will be beyond the understanding of men.
- Pray in the name of Jesus that God will have His way in your life.
- Pray in the name of Jesus that no storm, no drought or dark seasons will cause you to lose focus of God's word concerning your life.
- Thank the Lord for making you a blessing to your generation in Jesus name.

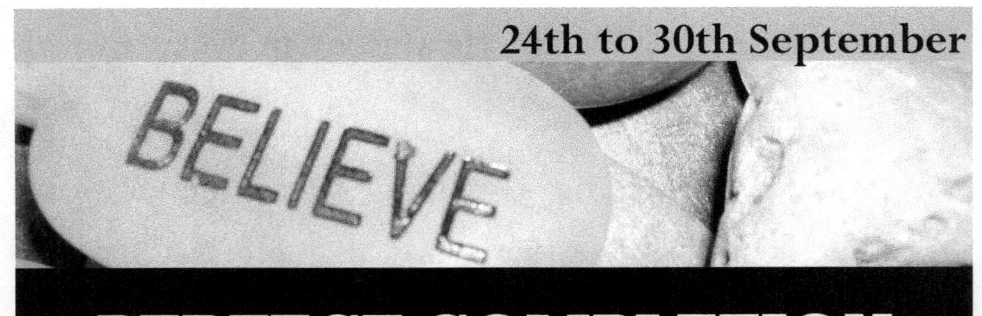

SCRIPTURE FOR THE WEEK

"Shall I bring to the time of birth, and not cause delivery?" says the Lord. "Shall I who cause delivery shut up the womb?" says your God." **Isaiah 66:9**

CONFESSION

- I believe and confess that I serve a faithful God. I declare that He who has begun a good work in my life will bring it to perfect completion.
- I decree today that what God has started in my life will not be delayed nor aborted. I confess that I will not miss my season of harvest.
- Today, I declare that God is bringing completion to every area of my life. I speak completion to any testimony that appears delayed in the name of Jesus.

- I speak completion to any breakthrough that appears to be suspended in my life in the name of Jesus.
- I confess that from this week my hope will turn to fulfilment, my prayer to praise and my waiting to a time of celebration.
- I declare today that I am blessed and highly favoured.

PRAYER POINTS FOR THE WEEK

- Pray in the name of Jesus that God will bring to perfect completion the good work He has begun in your life.
- Pray in the name of Jesus that what God has started in your life will not be delayed nor aborted.
- Pray in the name of Jesus that there will be perfect completion to any breakthrough that appears to be suspended in your life.
- Thank God that this week your hope will turn to fulfilment, your prayer to praise and your waiting to a time of celebration in Jesus name.

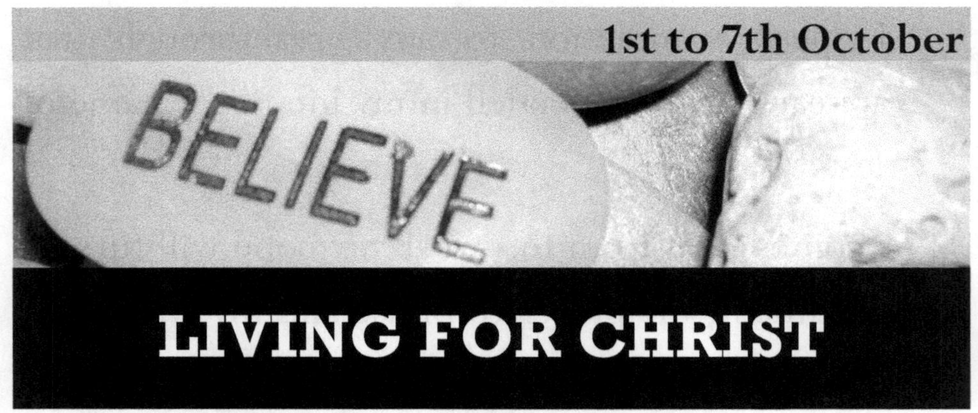

SCRIPTURE FOR THE WEEK

*"Likewise you also, reckon yourselves to be dead indeed to sin, but alive to God in Christ Jesus our Lord. Therefore do not let sin reign in your mortal body, that you should obey it in its lusts."***Romans 6:11-12**

CONFESSION

- I believe and confess that through Christ, I am a child of God. I confess today that my spirit is alive to God and my life is subject to His direction.
- I declare and confess that the fruit of the Spirit manifests in my life. By the grace of God, love and joy will manifest continually in my life. Goodness and peace is my portion in Jesus name.

- From this day onwards, I will be full of kindness and gentleness. I will be faithful in every area of my life, and I will exhibit self-control throughout my life.
- The grace of God will make me a person of peace and I will reflect the glory of God in my going out and coming in.
- I declare that I will be led by the Holy Spirit. I will be sensitive to the Holy Spirit. I will consciously walk in the Spirit and will have victory over the flesh in my life.
- I confess today that I am on my way to becoming a spiritual giant in the name of Jesus.
- I declare today that I am blessed and highly favoured.

PRAYER POINTS FOR THE WEEK

- Pray in the name of Jesus that at all time your spirit will be alive to God and your life subject to His direction.

- Pray in the name of Jesus that the fruit of the Spirit will manifest continually in your life.
- Pray in the name of Jesus that you will be led by the Holy Spirit at all times as you learn to be sensitive to the Him.
- Pray in the name of Jesus for the grace to consciously walk in the Spirit and to have victory over the flesh in your life.

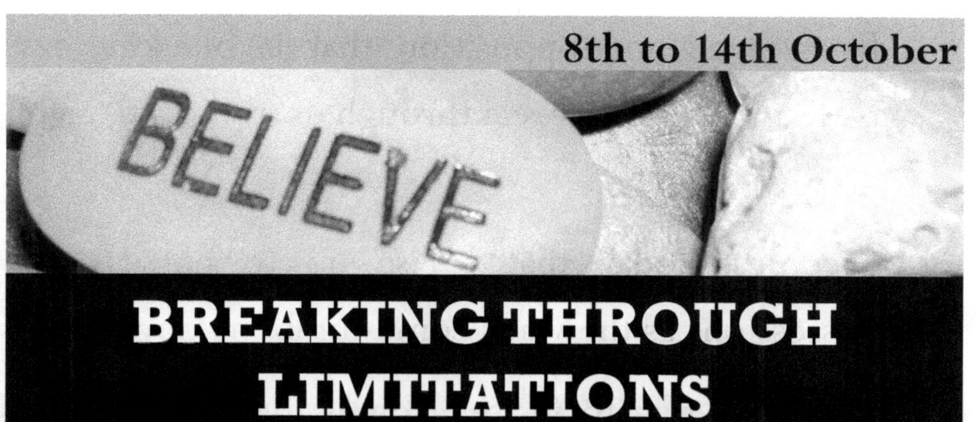

8th to 14th October

BREAKING THROUGH LIMITATIONS

SCRIPTURE FOR THE WEEK

" By faith the walls of Jericho fell down after they were encircled for seven days." **Hebrews 11:30**

CONFESSION

- I believe and confess that my God is a mighty Deliverer and the Lord of Hosts.
- I confess today that by faith, every wall of limitation has been broken in the name of Jesus.
- Every wall of limitation that has limited my spiritual growth has fallen in the name of Jesus.
- I declare today that the walls of opposition that has held me stagnant has come down now.
- The wall of opposition that is preventing me from entering my destiny is no more in Jesus' name.

- Every wall and opposition that is blocking my path to a major breakthrough is removed right now.
- I confess today that I rise up to possess my possessions as the walls come tumbling down.
- I take the territories due me as the opposition is destroyed in the name of Jesus.
- I declare today that every demonic delay in my life has ended today in the name of Jesus.
- I receive quick restoration of any losses that the delay has caused me in the name of Jesus.
- I declare today that I am blessed and highly favoured.

PRAYER POINTS FOR THE WEEK

- Command by faith, every wall of limitation to be broken in the name of Jesus.
- In the name of Jesus command every wall of limitation that has limited your spiritual growth to fall.
- Pray in the name of Jesus that the walls of

opposition that has held you stagnant will come down.

- Thank the Lord that the wall of opposition that is preventing you from entering your destiny is no more in Jesus' name.

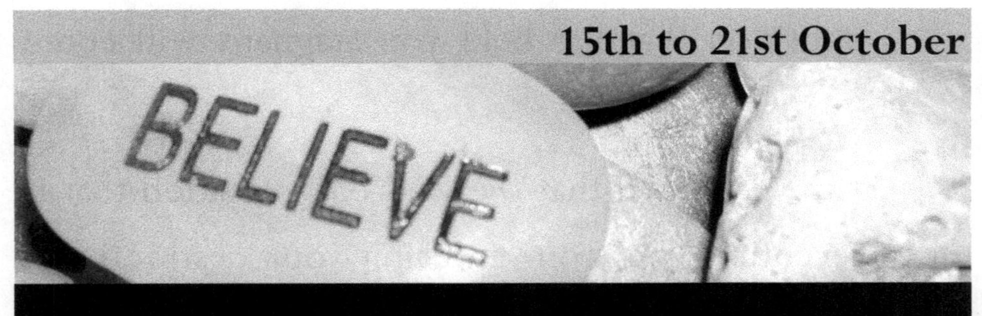

SCRIPTURE FOR THE WEEK

"Jesus said to him, "If you can believe, all things are possible to him who believes."" **Mark 9:23**

CONFESSION

- I believe and confess that all things are possible for me in the name of Jesus.
- I declare based on His word that the walls of doubt are falling off my life right now.
- I declare that from today, I will no longer be bound by doubt in the name of Jesus. I break every hold of doubt in my mind and set myself free from that limitation in Jesus' name.
- I confess that in spite of the negative circumstances I may face, God is faithful to do all that He has promised in my life.

- I declare that I have total victory over doubt in every area of my life.
- I confess that, that which men have declared impossible will be made possible for me. I will not miss my breakthrough and testimony in the name of Jesus.
- I hear the sound of rejoicing in my home in the name of Jesus. I see celebration in my life in the name of Jesus.
- I declare today that I am blessed and highly favoured.

PRAYER POINTS FOR THE WEEK

- Pray in the name of Jesus that from today, you will no longer be bound by doubt.
- In the name of Jesus break every hold of doubt in your mind and set yourself free from that limitation.
- Pray in the name of Jesus for a total victory over doubt in every area of your life.
- Thank the Lord that what men have declared impossible will be made possible for you.

SCRIPTURE FOR THE WEEK

"Through God we will do valiantly, For it is He who shall tread down our enemies." **Psalms 60:12**

CONFESSION

- I believe and confess that I serve a great and living God.
- I declare and decree that this is my season to do exploits. I confess that in this year, the Lord will help me to do the impossible.
- I declare that the Lord will open my eyes to see what He has in store for me. I refuse to be limited by what I see in the natural. In this year, I will live by faith and not by sight.

- I confess that my ears are open to hear the instructions from above. I will not be distracted by the noise around me. I declare that my ears will not miss God's instruction for me.
- I declare that my steps are ordered by God. In this season, I will not just follow what others are doing in the natural. I receive insight to take the unusual steps for unusual exploits.
- I confess that unusual exploits are mine in this season.
- I declare today that I am blessed and highly favoured.

PRAYER POINTS FOR THE WEEK

- Pray in the name of Jesus that in this year, the Lord will help you to do the impossible.
- Pray in the name of Jesus that the Lord will open your eyes to see what He has in store for you and refuse to be limited by what you see in the natural.

- Pray in the name of Jesus to receive insight to take the unusual steps for unusual exploits.
- Thank God that unusual exploits are yours in this season in Jesus name.

29th October to 4th November

EXPERIENCING OPEN HEAVENS

SCRIPTURE FOR THE WEEK

"The Lord will open to you His good treasure, the heavens, to give the rain to your land in its season, and to bless all the work of your hand. You shall lend to many nations, but you shall not borrow. And the Lord will make you the head and not the tail; you shall be above only, and not be beneath, if you heed the commandments of the Lord your God, which I command you today, and are careful to observe them."
Deuteronomy 28:12-13

CONFESSION

- In this month, I declare that God has opened the heavens over my life.
- My tithes and offerings are provoking unusual harvest into my life in the name of Jesus.

- I believe and confess that unusual testimonies are manifesting in my life right now in the name of Jesus.
- My story is changing for the better in the name of Jesus.
- My hands shall handle the fruit of God's blessing on my life.
- My mouth shall sing praise of new things He has done in my life.
- I believe and confess that divine intervention which will change my life forever is my portion right now.
- From today, I am a walking testimony in the name of Jesus.
- I declare today that I am blessed and highly favoured.

PRAYER POINTS FOR THE WEEK

- Pray in the name of Jesus that God will open the heavens over your life.

- Pray in the name of Jesus that your tithes and offerings will provoke unusual harvest into your life.
- Pray in the name of Jesus that as the heavens open over your life, your hands shall handle the fruit of God's blessing on your life.
- Thank the Lord that divine intervention which will change your life forever is your portion right now as the heaven opens over your life.

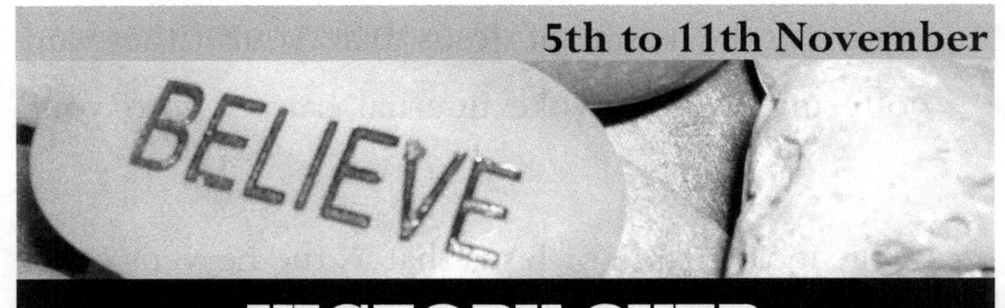

VICTORY OVER EVIL POLLUTION

SCRIPTURE FOR THE WEEK

"Keep your heart with all diligence, For out of it spring the issues of life." **Proverbs 4:23**

CONFESSION

- I believe and confess that I am ordained by God to be fruitful in every area of my life.
- I confess that my heart will be continually set on God and filled with His love.
- I declare that no scheme of the enemy will succeed in polluting my heart. I reject any attack of the devil on my relationship with God.
- I declare today that out of my life will come forth giftings that will bring glory to God.
- There will be overflow of testimonies in my life.

- Every attempt of the devil to pollute my testimony and blessing is cancelled right now, in the name of Jesus.
- I speak into the week ahead that harvest will meet harvest in my life; good news will follow good news.
- I will see God bringing completion to major matters in my life, in the name of Jesus.
- I declare today that I am blessed and highly favoured.

PRAYER POINTS FOR THE WEEK

- Pray in the name of Jesus that your heart will be continually set on God and filled with His love.
- Pray in the name of Jesus that no scheme of the enemy will succeed in polluting your heart.
- Pray in the name of Jesus that out of your life will come forth giftings that will bring glory to God.
- Thank the Lord that there will be overflow of testimonies in your life.

SCRIPTURE FOR THE WEEK

"Let your conduct be without covetousness; be content with such things as you have. For He Himself has said, "I will never leave you nor forsake you."" **Hebrews 13:5**

CONFESSION

- I believe and confess that, through Christ, I am the Light of the World. I receive grace to be a continuous light to the world around me.
- I declare today that the works of my hands will bear testimony of God's goodness in my life. Wherever I go, the favour of God will

  cause me to excel. I will make great impact wherever I find myself.

- The grace of God will cause me to resist any temptation to compromise.
- I declare today that I will not be conformed to this world.
- My transformation will be evident to all in Jesus name.
- I confess the rest of my days will be spent reflecting the glory of God in the name of Jesus.
- My spiritual life will glorify God.
- My business and career exploits will glorify God.
- My family life will bring glory to God.
- I receive grace to be a carrier of the anointing of God in every area of my life.
- I declare today that I am blessed and highly favoured.

PRAYER POINTS FOR THE WEEK

- Pray in the name of Jesus to receive grace to be a continuous light to the world around you.

- Pray in the name of Jesus that wherever you go, the favour of God will cause you to excel and make great impact wherever you find yourself.
- Pray in the name of Jesus that you will not be conformed to this world but your transformation will be evident to all.
- Thank the Lord that your spiritual life, family life, business and career exploits will glorify God.

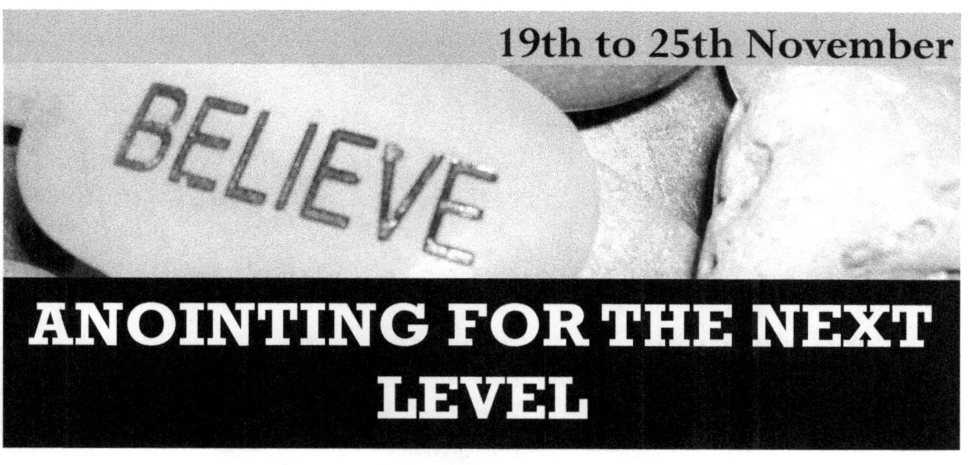

ANOINTING FOR THE NEXT LEVEL

SCRIPTURE FOR THE WEEK

"And as those who bore the ark came to the Jordan, and the feet of the priests who bore the ark dipped in the edge of the water (for the Jordan overflows all its banks during the whole time of harvest), that the waters which came down from upstream stood still, and rose in a heap very far away at Adam, the city that is beside Zaretan. So the waters that went down into the Sea of the Arabah, the Salt Sea, failed, and were cut off; and the people crossed over opposite Jericho."
Joshua 3:15-16

CONFESSION

- Today, I pray and declare that there will be an outbreak of miracles in my life in Jesus name. I confess today that testimonies will abound in my life from now on in the name of Jesus.

- I decree and declare over my life, that everything that has limited me is broken in the name of Jesus.
- Every battle that has held me at bay comes to an end right now in Jesus name.
- I receive grace and power to walk into the next phase of God's assignment for me in the name of Jesus.
- Every demonic delay is cancelled in the name of Jesus.
- I call into being answers to my prayer in the name of Jesus. I receive the full manifestation of whatever heaven has released for me in the name of Jesus.
- From today, I am a walking testimony.
- I declare today that I am blessed and highly favoured.

PRAYER POINTS FOR THE WEEK

- Pray in the name of Jesus that there will be an outbreak of miracles in your life.

- Pray that everything that has limited you will be broken.
- Pray in the name of Jesus that every battle that has held you at bay comes to an end right now.
- Thank the Lord that you have received grace and power to walk into the next phase of God's assignment for you in the name of Jesus.

SCRIPTURE FOR THE WEEK

"He has put a new song in my mouth-- Praise to our God; many will see it and fear, and will trust in the Lord." **Psalms 40:3**

CONFESSION

- I believe and confess that I serve a mighty God. The goodness and mercies of God follows me wherever I go.
- I declare today that no storm or challenge will rob me of my testimony. I confess that, through the grace of God, I will do unusual exploits in the name of Jesus.
- The story of my life will be a living testimony. From this day, my experiences in every area of my

life will reflect the glory of God. The fruits of my life will be supernatural.

- Excellence and overflow will follow everything that I set my hands to do.
- Testimonies from my life will cause my critics to change their minds concerning me. The breakthroughs in my life will cause even my enemies to acknowledge the goodness of God.
- I declare today that I am blessed and highly favoured.

PRAYER POINTS FOR THE WEEK

- Pray in the name of Jesus that no storm or challenge will rob you of your testimony as you keep trusting in the Lord.
- Pray in the name of Jesus that God will cause the fruits of your life to be supernatural as you trust in Him.
- Pray in the name of Jesus that testimonies from your life will cause your critics to change their minds concerning you.

- Thank the Lord that Breakthroughs in your life will cause even your enemies to acknowledge the goodness of God.

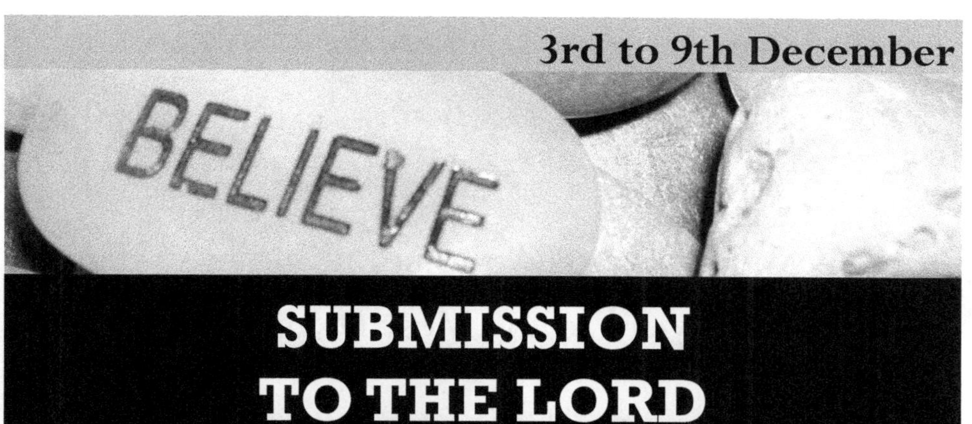

3rd to 9th December

SUBMISSION TO THE LORD

SCRIPTURE FOR THE WEEK

"And now, Israel, what does the Lord your God require of you, but to fear the Lord your God, to walk in all His ways and to love Him, to serve the Lord your God with all your heart and with all your soul." **Deuteronomy 10:12**

CONFESSION

- I believe and confess that the God I serve is a holy God. There is none like Him and there is no one that can be compared to Him

- I confess today that the fear of the Lord will never depart from my life and from that of my children. I decree that no deception, no challenge or opposition will cause me to stray from the ways of God.

- My love for God will never wax cold and my

hunger and thirst for Him will never cease. I declare today that I will serve The Lord all the days of my life.

- I speak to everything within me and everything in my life to yield to the Most High in the name of Jesus.
- I declare today that I am blessed and highly favoured.

PRAYER POINTS FOR THE WEEK

- Pray in the name of Jesus that the fear of the Lord will never depart from your life and from that of your children.
- Pray in the name of Jesus that no deception, no challenge or opposition will cause you to stray from the ways of God.
- Pray in the name of Jesus that your love for God will never wax cold and your hunger and thirst for Him will never cease.
- Pray in the name of Jesus that everything within you and everything in your life will yield to the Most High.

SCRIPTURE FOR THE WEEK

"And the remnant who have escaped of the house of Judah Shall again take root downward, And bear fruit upward." **2 Kings 19:30**

CONFESSION

- I believe and confess that from today, the power of God overshadows me.
- I declare and decree that every limitation in my life is broken in Jesus name.
- Chains are falling off in every area of my life.
- I confess that I am entering a season of fruitfulness now.
- Every area of my life will bear fruit.

- My spiritual life will bear fruit, my family life will be a testimony, my business and career will experience divine increase in the name of Jesus.
- I declare today that God has brought me into a wealthy place. The power of lack is broken in my life in Jesus name.
- From today, I confess that wealth and riches shall be in my house and my generation shall be blessed.
- I confess that I receive a new anointing to usher me into a new season.
- A season in which, I will do as occasion serves me.
- I move into divine success without toil and sweat in the name of Jesus.
- I declare today that I am blessed and highly favoured.

PRAYER POINTS FOR THE WEEK

- Pray in the name of Jesus that the Lord will usher you into your season of fruitfulness.

- Pray in the name of Jesus that every area of my life will bear fruit.
- Pray in the name of Jesus that your spiritual life will bear fruit, your family life will be a testimony, your business and career will experience divine increase.
- Thank the Lord that wealth and riches shall be in your house and your generation shall be blessed in Jesus name.

17th to 23rd December

FROM MOURNING INTO DANCING

SCRIPTURE FOR THE WEEK

"Then you shall know that I am the Lord, when I have opened your graves, O My people, and brought you up from your graves. I will put My Spirit in you, and you shall live, and I will place you in your own land. Then you shall know that I, the Lord, have spoken it and performed it," says the Lord.'"
Ezekiel 37:13-14

CONFESSION

- I believe and confess that my God reigns above all. He is above all and there is none like Him.
- I confess today that by faith, every dead situation in my life is coming back to life in the name of Jesus.

- To every dead situation in my life right now, I speak the word of God and I declare that the life of God will manifest in it now in Jesus name.
- I confess today that my life will not be a tragedy.
- I declare that even in areas of my life where the experts have declared dead, I receive life right now in Jesus name.
- I declare today that in situations where the sympathizers have gathered to mourn with me, my mourning shall be turned into dancing in the name of Jesus.
- I confess that my tests and tribulations will result in testimonies!
- My battles will result in victories! My waiting will result in fulfilment in the name of Jesus.
- I declare today that I am blessed and highly favoured.

PRAYER POINTS FOR THE WEEK

- Pray in the name of Jesus that every dead situation in your life will come back to life.

- Pray in the name of Jesus that areas of your life where the experts have declared dead, will receive life right now.
- Pray in the name of Jesus that in situations where the sympathisers have gathered to mourn with you, your mourning shall be turned into dancing.
- Thank God that your tests and tribulations will result in testimonies! Your battles will result in victories! Your waiting will result in fulfilment in the name of Jesus.

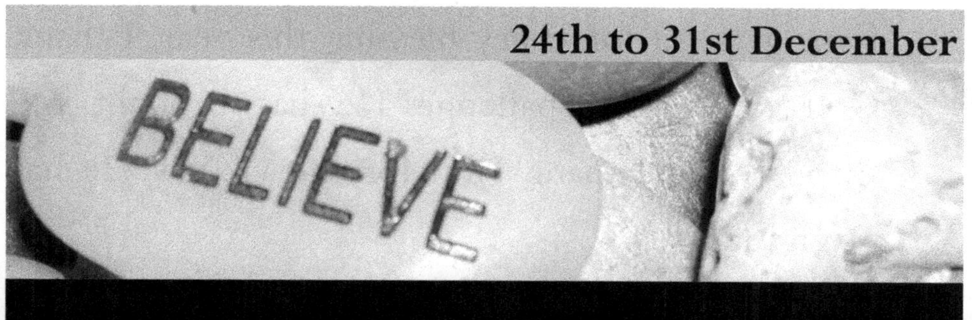

SCRIPTURE FOR THE WEEK

" I will bless the Lord at all times; His praise shall continually be in my mouth." **Psalms 34:1**

CONFESSION

- I believe and confess that I serve a good God. His mercies endure forever in my life.
- I thank the Lord for bringing me through this year and I confess that songs of celebration and thanksgiving will not cease in my life, in the name of Jesus.
- I declare and decree that the Lord will crown this year with a great testimony in my life.
- I receive a mighty manifestation in my life before this year ends, in the name of Jesus.

- I am grateful for every blessing this year, I thank God for every challenge He has brought me through and I thank Him for the victory He has given me.
- I declare today that I will not run out of reasons to be thankful to God.
- The Lord will give me many more reasons to celebrate in the year to come.
- I declare today that I am blessed and highly favoured.

PRAYER POINTS FOR THE WEEK

- Pray in the name of Jesus that songs of celebration and thanksgiving will not cease in your life as you bless the Lord at all times.
- Pray in the name of Jesus that the Lord will crown this year with a great testimony in your life as you bless Him.
- Bless and thank God for every challenge He has brought you through and thank Him for the victory He has given.

- Pray in the name of Jesus that the Lord will give you many more reasons to celebrate in the year to come as you bless Him.

OTHER BOOK BY ANDY YAWSON

I Believe and Confess

KNOWING AND CONFESSING HIS WORD

VOLUME 1

52

Key Scriptures

Bible-based Confessions

Sets of Prayer Topics

Weeks of Victory this year!

ANDY YAWSON

Paperback and Kindle versions of Andy Yawson's books are available on www.amazon.com

Or contact the author by email at illumination_house@yahoo.com

www.ingramcontent.com/pod-product-compliance
Lightning Source LLC
Chambersburg PA
CBHW060325050426
42449CB00011B/2653

* 9 7 8 9 9 8 8 2 0 7 9 1 5 *